Elon Musk - The Biography

A Visionary's Journey

Stellar Stories

Contents

Chapter One

Seeds of Innovation

Innovation often stems from a curiosity and a desire to push boundaries, and Elon Musk's journey is no exception. Born on June 28, 1971, in Pretoria, South Africa, Musk demonstrated a natural inclination towards innovation from a young age.

Growing up, Musk was an avid reader, often immersing himself in the realms of science fiction and fantasy novels. These imaginative stories ignited a spark within him, nurturing his creativity and inspiring him to dream big. Musk's early exposure to these fantastical worlds laid the foundation for his vision of a future filled with technological advancements and possibilities that seemed unimaginable to others.

But it wasn't just the pages of books that fueled Musk's imagination. His parents, Maye and Errol Musk, played a crucial role in shaping his innovative mindset. Maye, a professional dietitian and model, instilled in him the importance of seeking knowledge and exploring his interests. Meanwhile, Errol, an electromechanical engineer, introduced Musk to the world of machinery, electronics, and the intricacies of how things work. Combining his parents' influences with his own insatiable curiosity, Elon embarked on a journey of discovery and invention.

At the age of twelve, Musk encountered his first computer, the Commodore VIC-20. This encounter was a watershed moment for young Musk as his fascination with technology was ignited. He dove headfirst into the world of programming, teaching himself how to code and exploring the vast potential of computers. Musk would spend countless hours absorbed in the world of zeros and ones, fueled by the limitless possibilities that technology offered.

This early exposure to the power of technology further fueled Musk's passion for innovation and set him on a course towards shaping the future of humanity. He began to see the potential of utilizing technology not only for personal enjoyment but also as a tool to solve some of the world's most pressing problems.

As a teenager, Musk exhibited his entrepreneurial spirit by launching his first business venture, a video game called Blastar. While the game may have been rudimentary by today's standards, the fact that Musk was able to create and sell it successfully at the age of seventeen was a testament to his determination and ingenuity. It was an early indication of his ability to identify opportunities and transform ideas into reality.

After completing his studies in South Africa, Musk realized that if he truly wanted to make a significant impact, he needed to be in the heart of technological innovation. In 1995, armed with just a few thousand dollars and an unwavering belief in his vision, Musk made the bold decision to move to California's Silicon Valley – a breeding ground for pioneering startups and tech giants.

Chapter Two

Childhood Dreams and Early Endeavors

E lon's journey towards becoming an innovative entrepreneur and visionary leader began in his childhood. Even as a young boy growing up in Pretoria, South Africa, Musk displayed an insatiable curiosity and a unique ability to think outside the box.

From an early age, Musk was fascinated by technology and dreamed of creating something revolutionary. As a child, he would spend hours reading science fiction novels, immersing himself in futuristic tales of exploration, invention, and human resilience. These stories ignited his imagination and fueled his ambition to one day make those dreams a reality.

Musk's parents recognized his exceptional intellectual abilities and enrolled him in Waterkloof House Preparatory School, where he quickly stood out as a prodigious student. He consumed books at an astonishing rate, devouring knowledge on a wide range of subjects, from mathematics and physics to computer science. Musk's hunger for knowledge was insatiable, and he would often spend hours deep in thought, contemplating the mysteries of the universe and pondering the possibilities that lay beyond.

At the age of 12, Musk developed his first computer game, a space-themed adventure that garnered attention from local software developers. This early success not only showcased his technical skills but also revealed his ability to create something that captured people's imaginations. It was a glimpse into his future as an entrepreneur and innovator.

Musk's entrepreneurial spirit and determination did not stop there. By the time he was a teenager, he had already started several small businesses, displaying a shrewd understanding of market demand and a knack for identifying opportunities. From selling video game strategies to developing and selling software for the financial sector, Musk was constantly seeking opportunities to create and innovate.

One of his earliest endeavors was a company called Zip2, which aimed to revolutionize the way newspapers delivered business directories and maps to customers. Musk's vision was to digitize and streamline this process, allowing users to easily locate businesses and get directions. His relentless pursuit of success led him to secure partnerships with major newspapers, and Zip2 quickly grew in popularity. This venture not only provided him with valuable experience but also set the stage for his future entrepreneurial endeavors.

With a taste of success under his belt, Musk set his sights on even more audacious goals. Inspired by his childhood dreams of space exploration, he co-founded SpaceX, a private aerospace manufacturer and space transportation company. Musk's vision was to make space travel more accessible and affordable, opening up new possibilities for human colonization of other planets. He believed that ensuring humanity's future was not confined to Earth was of vital importance, and he dedicated his resources and energy to achieving this vision.

Simultaneously, Musk also embarked on a new venture: Tesla Motors. Frustrated with the lack of viable electric cars in the market, Musk sought to disrupt the automotive industry by creating high-performance, electric vehicles. Despite facing numerous challenges and skepticism from the industry, Musk pursued his vision relentlessly, eventually revolutionizing the electric vehicle market and paving the way for a greener future.

Musk's determination, however, came with sacrifices. In the early years of SpaceX and Tesla, he poured nearly all of his personal fortune into the companies, risking financial ruin in pursuit of his grand visions. Musk faced many obstacles along the way, but his unwavering belief in his goals and his unwavering work ethic propelled him forward.

Chapter Three

The Birth of Zip2: Musk's First Taste of Entrepreneurship

In the late 1990s, a young Elon Musk embarked on his first entrepreneurial venture: Zip2. This company would lay the foundation for his future success and serve as a testament to his relentless drive and innovative thinking.

Born out of Musk's desire to capitalize on the emerging internet boom, Zip2 aimed to revolutionize the way local businesses advertised and interacted with consumers. The company developed software that allowed newspapers to create online directories seamlessly, providing users with accurate and up-to-date information about local businesses.

Musk recognized that the internet held tremendous potential for transforming numerous industries, and he saw an opportunity in helping traditional media outlets adapt to the digital age. In 1995, he co-founded Zip2 with his brother Kimbal Musk and a small team of talented engineers.

At the outset, Zip2 faced significant challenges. The internet was still relatively new, and many businesses were slow to embrace its potential. Musk and his team had to convince skeptical newspaper executives that their software was not just a passing fad but a viable solution. They hit the streets, pitching Zip2's services to newspaper publishers across the country.

Their persistence paid off. Zip2 secured partnerships with major newspapers like The New York Times and The Chicago Tribune, cementing its position as a leading provider of online business directories. The company's innovative technology and commitment to customer satisfaction set it apart from competitors.

As Zip2 gained traction, Musk's ambition grew. He envisioned expanding beyond local directories and transforming Zip2 into a full-fledged online platform for city guides, complete with mapping and directory services. This vision attracted the attention of major investors, including venture capital firms and notable angel investors.

With funding secured, Zip2 continued to grow rapidly. The company expanded its operations worldwide, establishing partnerships with newspapers in Europe, Australia, and Asia. Musk's leadership and entrepreneurial spirit were evident as he steered Zip2 through various hurdles and positioned it as a leader in the digital advertising space.

One of the key factors behind Zip2's success was Musk's ability to forge strategic partnerships. Early on, he recognized the importance of collaborating with established media outlets to reach a wider audience and gain credibility. Zip2's partnership with The New York Times, in particular, was a game-changer, as it brought their services to a vast readership and solidified their position in the market.

Furthermore, Musk's relentless focus on ensuring customer satisfaction set Zip2 apart from its competitors. He understood that the success of their platform relied on providing accurate and valuable information to users, and he implemented strict quality control measures to maintain the integrity of their online directories. Through constant innovation and listening to customer feedback, Zip2 evolved into a trusted source for local business information.

In 1999, Compaq Computer Corporation recognized the value of Zip2's technology and acquired the company for $307 million. This marked a significant milestone for Musk, as it was his first major financial success. The sale of Zip2 not only provided him with a significant windfall but also validated his ability to build and sell a successful tech startup.

Looking back, the birth of Zip2 represented a pivotal moment in Elon Musk's entrepreneurial journey. It laid the groundwork for his future ventures, showcasing his ability to identify opportunities in emerging industries and solve complex problems through innovative technology. Zip2 taught Musk valuable lessons about scaling a business, securing partnerships, and navigating the fast-paced world of technology startups.

The success of Zip2 fueled Musk's ambition and set the stage for his next groundbreaking venture: X.com, which would ultimately evolve into the widely-used online payment system, PayPal. With each new endeavor, Musk continued to push boundaries, change industries, and leave an indelible mark on the world of entrepreneurship. His experiences with Zip2 shaped his future decisions, as he understood the importance of building innovative solutions, establishing strategic partnerships, and prioritizing customer satisfaction.

As Musk reflects on his journey with Zip2, he acknowledges that the entrepreneurial path is not without its challenges. It often requires unwavering determination, a willingness to take risks, and a relentless pursuit of excellence. Through Zip2, he learned the significance of adaptability and the importance of being nimble in a constantly evolving industry.

Zip2 not only served as a stepping stone for Musk but also left a lasting impact on the advertising and media landscape. Its innovative approach to local business directories foreshadowed the rise of digital platforms that would eventually disrupt traditional media models. Musk's ability to see the potential in emerging technologies and adapt them to existing industries would become a hallmark of his entrepreneurial career.

The lessons learned from Zip2 continue to shape Musk's ventures today, as he seeks to revolutionize space travel with SpaceX, make electric vehicles mainstream with Tesla, and spearhead the development of sustainable energy solutions with companies like SolarCity and Tesla

Energy. Elon Musk's journey as an entrepreneur is an ongoing story of fearless innovation, underscoring his commitment to pushing the boundaries of what is believed to be possible.

Chapter Four

X.com and the Birth of PayPal: Revolutionizing the Online Payment Industry

In the late 1990s, Elon Musk embarked on a new venture that would forever change the landscape of online payments. It all began with X.com, an online payment company founded by Musk in March 1999. The idea behind X.com was to create a digital wallet that would enable users to securely make payments and transfers online.

Musk recognized the potential of the internet and saw a future where online transactions would become increasingly common. However, at the time, the online payment industry was fragmented and lacked a seamless and universally accepted platform. Musk aimed to rev-olutionize this space by providing a simple, secure, and convenient solution.

X.com quickly gained traction and grew in popularity due to its inno-vative approach. The platform allowed users to send and receive pay-ments via email, providing a level of convenience that was previously unheard of in the industry. Additionally, X.com integrated its system with Palm handheld devices, further expanding its reach and catering to the growing demand for mobile payments.

As X.com rapidly gained momentum, it faced competition from an-other company known as Confinity, which was offering a similar on-line payment service called PayPal. Recognizing the synergy between the two companies, Musk proposed a merger in March 2000, and X.com acquired Confinity, bringing together the best of both platforms.

Under Musk's leadership, the newly merged company decided to adopt the name PayPal, as it resonated more with users and encom-passed the essence of their vision. This decision proved to be pivotal in establishing PayPal as a household name in the online payment industry.

PayPal flourished under Musk's guidance, focusing not only on user experience but also on security. Musk was adamant about creating a platform that people could trust with their financial information, and PayPal implemented stringent security measures to protect users' data and transactions.

One of the key factors that propelled PayPal's success was its integration with eBay, a prominent online marketplace. PayPal became the preferred payment method for eBay users, streamlining the buying and selling process and establishing itself as the go-to payment solution for online transactions within the eBay ecosystem.

Beyond eBay, PayPal expanded its reach and became widely accepted by various online merchants and businesses. The convenience and security offered by PayPal attracted both consumers and sellers alike, propelling the company's exponential growth. PayPal continuously worked on improving its user interface and streamlining the payment process, ensuring a seamless experience for its users.

In addition to its user-friendly interface, PayPal implemented various fraud protection mechanisms, ensuring a safe environment for users' transactions. The company invested in cutting-edge technology and sophisticated algorithms to detect and prevent fraudulent activities, giving users peace of mind. This emphasis on security and trust set PayPal apart from its competitors, fueling its reputation as a reliable and dependable payment platform.

As PayPal's success skyrocketed, the company went public in 2002, making its initial public offering (IPO) on the NASDAQ stock exchange. This move not only provided PayPal with increased capital but also positioned it as a leading player in the online payment industry. Musk's strategic vision and the dedication of the PayPal team to continuously innovate and provide exceptional service to its users proved to be a winning combination.

However, PayPal's journey was not without challenges. The company faced numerous legal and regulatory hurdles, including concerns over money laundering and fraud prevention. PayPal diligently worked hand in hand with regulatory bodies, implementing robust compliance measures to ensure that the platform adhered to the necessary requirements. This commitment to responsibility and transparency not only allowed PayPal to navigate through legal complexities but also positioned it as a trusted financial institution.

In October 2002, eBay recognized the potential of PayPal and acquired it for $1.5 billion, making it the preferred payment method for all eBay transactions. This acquisition further solidified PayPal's position as a leading player in the online payment industry, with Musk serving as a member of PayPal's board of directors.

The birth of PayPal not only revolutionized online payments but also laid the foundation for Musk's future endeavors. It proved that he had the entrepreneurial prowess and vision to disrupt industries with innovative solutions. The success of PayPal provided Musk with the financial resources and credibility to pursue his grand ambitions, such as space exploration and electric vehicles.

The experience gained from PayPal influenced Musk's approach to business strategy and shaped his subsequent ventures. One of the key lessons learned was the importance of building scalable and sustainable business models. Musk realized that to create lasting impact, companies need to focus on long-term vision and profitability rather than short-term gains. This mindset resonates throughout his ventures, from Tesla's relentless pursuit of creating cutting-edge electric vehicles to SpaceX's mission to revolutionize space travel.

Furthermore, PayPal's success paved the way for the development of other online payment platforms and the broader acceptance of digital transactions. The advent of PayPal triggered a shift in consumer behavior, fostering a newfound trust in online payments and driving the exponential growth of e-commerce. Today, PayPal continues to be a dominant player in the online payment space, continuously innovating and evolving to meet the changing needs of its users.

In conclusion, the story of X.com and the birth of PayPal is a testament to Musk's ability to identify gaps in industries and create solutions that revolutionize the status quo. It marked the beginning of a remarkable journey for Musk, paving the way for his future endeavors that continue to push the boundaries of innovation and redefine industries. PayPal's impact on the online payment industry and its lasting legacy will forever be tied to Musk's entrepreneurial spirit and vision.

Chapter Five

SpaceX Takes Flight: Launching Rockets and Revolutionizing Space Travel

E lon step into the world of space travel started with the establishment of SpaceX, short for Space Exploration Technologies Corp. Founded in 2002, SpaceX set out to revolutionize the space industry by making space exploration more affordable and accessible.

The first major breakthrough for SpaceX came in 2008 with the successful launch of their Falcon 1 rocket. This marked the first privately-funded liquid-fueled vehicle to reach orbit. Prior to this historic achievement, space exploration had been dominated by government agencies such as NASA.

Building on the success of Falcon 1, Musk's team went on to develop the Falcon 9 rocket. This next-generation rocket was designed to be fully reusable, a groundbreaking concept in the aerospace industry. Reusability was essential to Musk's vision of drastically reducing launch costs and making space travel economically viable.

In 2012, SpaceX made history once again by becoming the first privately-funded company to dock a spacecraft, the Dragon, with the International Space Station (ISS). This achievement solidified SpaceX's position as a frontrunner in the race to commercialize space travel.

The year 2015 marked another significant milestone with the successful landing of the Falcon 9 first stage booster. This marked the first-ever landing of a rocket stage vertically, paving the way for reusable rockets that could drastically reduce the cost of space travel. A fully reusable rocket would make space missions more affordable and open up new opportunities for research, exploration, and even colonization of other planets.

Inspired by his childhood dream of reaching Mars, Musk unveiled the plans for the Interplanetary Transport System (ITS), later renamed Starship. The Starship is a fully reusable spacecraft designed to transport large numbers of people and cargo to destinations beyond Earth, including Mars. Musk envisions establishing a self-sustaining colony on Mars, making humanity a multi-planetary species.

SpaceX's continued advancements in rocket technology and their successful commercial launches have disrupted the space industry. By offering competitive pricing and reusable rockets, SpaceX has challenged the traditional players in the space sector, driving down costs and sparking innovation.

The development of the Starship has, in particular, captured the imagination of the world. With a height of 120 meters and a capacity to carry over 100 metric tons of cargo, this colossal spacecraft holds the promise of a new era for space exploration. The Starship aims to revolutionize transportation not just between Earth and Mars but also within our own planet.

To achieve this, SpaceX is also developing the Super Heavy rocket, which will act as the booster for the Starship. The Super Heavy rocket will feature a mind-boggling 31 Raptor engines, making it one of the most powerful rockets ever built. This two-stage system will be capable of delivering payloads to orbit in unprecedented quantities and will play a crucial role in future missions to Mars and beyond.

Beyond its achievements in space travel, SpaceX has also been instrumental in the development of satellite constellations. Under the Starlink project, SpaceX aims to deploy thousands of small satellites into low Earth orbit to provide global broadband internet coverage. This ambitious venture has the potential to bridge the digital divide and connect remote areas around the world.

Moreover, SpaceX's commitment to reusability has had a significant impact. By recovering and refurbishing rocket stages, the company has not only saved substantial costs but also demonstrated the feasibility of sustainable space travel. Reusability has become a core tenet of future space missions, with other companies and space agencies now working to incorporate this concept into their own rocket designs.

Additionally, SpaceX's success has reinvigorated public interest in space exploration. The company's live-streamed launches and daring experiments, such as launching Musk's personal Tesla Roadster into space, have captivated audiences worldwide and inspired a new generation of scientists, engineers, and dreamers.

As SpaceX accelerates the development and testing of the Starship, we can only imagine the transformative impact it will have on our understanding of the universe and our place within it. The dreams of colonizing Mars and becoming a multi-planetary civilization are no longer distant fantasies but tangible possibilities.

The journey of SpaceX is a testament to the power of determination, ambition, and thinking beyond the confines of conventional wisdom. As Elon Musk and his team continue to inspire the world with their groundbreaking endeavors, the future of space exploration holds tremendous promise, and SpaceX remains at the forefront of this exciting frontier.

With each successful launch and groundbreaking achievement, SpaceX continues to push the boundaries of what is possible, bringing us closer to a future where space travel is not just limited to astronauts but accessible to everyone. It is through endeavors like SpaceX that humanity's quest for knowledge and exploration continues to evolve, igniting our collective imagination and reminding us of the vast possibilities that lie beyond the confines of our home planet.

Chapter Six

Tesla Motors: Rethinking the Electric Vehicle Industry

In the early 2000s, as concerns about climate change and the dependency on fossil fuels continued to grow, Elon Musk set his sights on revolutionizing the automotive industry. He believed that electric vehicles (EVs) were the future of transportation and that it was time to bring them to the masses. This marked the birth of Tesla Motors.

Musk knew that in order to challenge the existing automotive giants, he needed to create a vehicle that was not only environmentally friendly but also desirable and high-performing. Tesla Motors' first offering, the Tesla Roadster, was a groundbreaking achievement. It was an all-electric sports car capable of going from 0 to 60 mph in under four seconds, with a range of over 200 miles. The roadster's success not only proved that EVs could be fast and powerful but also brought attention to the potential of electric vehicles.

However, Musk's vision extended far beyond creating a luxurious electric sports car. He aimed to disrupt the entire industry by pushing EVs into the mainstream market. To achieve this, Tesla Motors needed to develop more affordable models that appealed to a wider range of consumers.

This led to the production of the Tesla Model S, a sleek and high-performance sedan that quickly gained popularity among luxury vehicle enthusiasts. The Model S boasted impressive range capabilities, with the option for a larger battery pack that could achieve over 300 miles on a single charge. It also offered features such as Autopilot, which allowed for semi-autonomous driving, putting Tesla at the forefront of automotive technology.

One of the biggest challenges Musk faced was overcoming the limitations of conventional EVs, particularly the issue of range anxiety. To address this, Tesla invested heavily in developing a comprehensive network of Superchargers – fast-charging stations strategically placed along major travel routes. The Supercharger network enabled Tesla owners to travel long distances and recharge their vehicles quickly, effectively alleviating range anxiety and making EVs more practical for everyday use.

Beyond its vehicles, Tesla's impact on the automotive industry extends to its battery technology. The company recognized early on that battery advancements were critical to the success and affordability of electric vehicles. To overcome this obstacle, Musk spearheaded the construction of the Gigafactory, an expansive lithium-ion battery production facility in Nevada. With its vertical integration approach, Tesla managed to significantly reduce the cost of batteries by producing them at scale. This breakthrough not only made electric vehicles more accessible but also had a ripple effect on other industries, such as renewable energy storage, as the Gigafactory began supplying batteries for residential and commercial energy storage solutions.

Building on the success of the Model S, Tesla introduced the more affordable Model 3, aiming to bring EVs to the mass market. This ambitious project captured global attention, with hundreds of thousands of pre-orders flooding in within days of its announcement. The Model 3's affordability and impressive range, starting at 250 miles on a single charge, made it an attractive option for a broader range of consumers, further solidifying Tesla's position as a leading force in the electric vehicle industry.

Tesla's achievements have forced other manufacturers to accelerate their electric vehicle development efforts. Traditional automakers, initially dismissive of EVs, have realized the importance of adapting to the changing landscape and keeping up with Tesla's innovations. As a result, we have witnessed an influx of electric offerings from established automakers, who are now racing to catch up with Tesla's advancements.

But Tesla Motors' impact extends beyond just pushing for electric vehicles; the company has taken a holistic approach to sustainability. In addition to its electric vehicles and battery technology, Tesla ventured into the solar energy industry with its acquisition of SolarCity, a leading provider of solar energy systems. This move allowed Tesla to integrate solar power generation with its energy storage solutions, complementing its vision of sustainable transportation and energy solutions.

Musk's relentless pursuit of innovation and his commitment to sustainability have not only reimagined the electric vehicle industry but have also shaped public perception of what electric vehicles can be. Tesla Motors continues to push the boundaries of EV technology, with ongoing developments in autonomous driving, energy storage, and solar power solutions. With each new model, Tesla strives to improve the performance, affordability, and accessibility of electric vehicles while promoting a cleaner and more sustainable future for transportation.

The impact of Tesla Motors' groundbreaking achievements cannot be understated. With its visionary leader and passion for innovation, the company has sparked a global shift towards electric vehicles, inspiring both consumers and the automotive industry as a whole to rethink the future of transportation.

Chapter Seven

SolarCity and Renewable Energy: Powering a Sustainable Future

Renewable energy has gained increasing attention and importance in recent years due to its potential to address environmental concerns and reduce reliance on fossil fuels. In this chapter, we explore how Elon Musk played a significant role in advancing the renewable energy industry through his involvement with SolarCity.

SolarCity, founded in 2006 by Elon Musk's cousins Lyndon and Peter Rive, emerged as a key player in the solar energy sector, thanks to its innovative business model and mission to accelerate the adoption of clean, renewable energy sources such as solar power. Musk recognized the potential of solar energy as a scalable and sustainable solution to power the future, and SolarCity became a manifestation of his vision.

One of the major barriers to widespread adoption of solar energy was the high upfront cost of installing solar panels. SolarCity addressed this issue by pioneering a unique financial model called solar leasing. Under this model, customers were able to have solar panels installed on their premises without any upfront costs. Instead, they would sign a long-term power purchase agreement (PPA) to buy the energy generated by the solar panels at a fixed rate, often lower than traditional utility rates.

Solar leasing revolutionized the solar energy industry by making it accessible and affordable for homeowners, businesses, and communities. The financial burden was lifted, and more individuals and organizations could participate in the clean energy transition. SolarCity's success in implementing this innovative financing approach paved the way for other companies to adopt similar models, contributing to the exponential growth of the solar energy industry.

Furthermore, SolarCity expanded its reach beyond residential installations to venture into the commercial and utility-scale sectors. Recognizing the potential for solar energy to reshape the energy landscape, Musk envisioned a decentralized energy grid powered by widespread solar panel installations. This vision aligned with his broader mission to eliminate carbon emissions and combat climate change.

While SolarCity experienced rapid growth, it faced challenges from traditional utility companies and policy barriers. Musk's determination, however, led him to rally support from policymakers and investors, propelling the company forward. SolarCity became a leader in the renewable energy sector, making significant contributions to the transition to clean energy.

In 2016, SolarCity merged with Tesla, further solidifying Elon Musk's vision for an integrated sustainable future. The merger allowed Tesla to combine its expertise in energy storage with SolarCity's solar technologies, creating a comprehensive solution for renewable energy generation and storage.

With the merger, Tesla introduced the Powerwall, a home battery storage system that can store excess solar energy generated during the day for use during non-sunlight hours. This development not only helped overcome the intermittency challenge of solar power but also paved the way for greater energy independence for individuals and communities.

Moreover, Tesla's Gigafactory played a crucial role in the renewables ecosystem by producing lithium-ion batteries at an unprecedented scale. These advanced battery technologies not only power electric vehicles but also store energy generated from renewable sources, enabling a seamless transition towards a sustainable energy future.

Elon Musk's commitment to renewable energy extends far beyond SolarCity and Tesla. His groundbreaking ventures, such as the Boring Company and Neuralink, also have implications for the renewable energy landscape. The Boring Company's tunneling technology could potentially facilitate the laying of underground utility lines, ensuring efficient distribution of renewable energy to various regions. Neuralink's development of brain-computer interfaces could contribute to improving the energy efficiency of infrastructure and appliances, further reducing the carbon footprint.

Musk's drive to address climate change and create a sustainable future has inspired individuals and organizations worldwide to join the renewable energy revolution. His advocacy for aggressive climate action and his outspokenness on social media platforms have helped raise awareness about the urgency of transitioning to clean energy sources. Musk's influence extends beyond his own companies, as he has encouraged other businesses and entrepreneurs to embrace and invest in renewable energy solutions.

Looking ahead, Musk's vision for renewable energy remains ambitious. His pursuit of innovation has led him to explore the potential of other renewable sources such as wind and geothermal energy. Tesla's acquisition of SolarCity also hinted at the possibility of integrating solar technology into other facets of everyday life, from solar roof tiles to solar-powered electric vehicle charging stations.

In conclusion, SolarCity, under the guidance of Elon Musk, revolutionized the solar energy industry with its innovative financial model and commitment to making solar power accessible to all. The company's merger with Tesla and the introduction of energy storage solutions have further solidified Musk's vision for a sustainable future powered by renewable energy. SolarCity's impact continues to shape the renewable energy landscape, inspiring a global movement towards a cleaner, greener, and more sustainable future.

Hyperloop and The Boring Company: Reshaping Transportation Infrastructure

As Musk's revolutionary ideas continued to reshape industries, his vision for transportation infrastructure took center stage with the conception of the Hyperloop and The Boring Company.

The idea of the Hyperloop emerged in 2013 when Musk published a white paper titled "Hyperloop Alpha." This visionary document outlined a high-speed transportation system that would use low-pressure tubes to transport pods at near-supersonic speeds. With the potential to revolutionize intercity travel, Musk envisioned a future where passengers could travel from one city to another in a matter of minutes, reducing travel times dramatically.

Musk's motivation for the Hyperloop came from his frustration with existing transportation systems, which he considered both slow and inefficient. He believed that by combining elements of air hockey, magnetic levitation, and vacuum tubes, he could create a transportation system that would be not only incredibly fast but also cost-effective and sustainable. The Hyperloop concept aimed to minimize air resistance, pushing the pods through low-pressure tubes with magnetic levitation and using a linear induction motor to achieve speeds of up to 760 mph (1,220 km/h).

While Musk himself did not take the lead in developing the Hyperloop, his vision inspired numerous individuals and companies to explore its potential. The ability to transport people and cargo at unprecedented speeds while reducing the environmental impact generated immense interest worldwide. Competitions were organized, attracting engineering teams from around the world who were eager to design and build prototype Hyperloop pods. These competitions served as incubators for innovation, fostering cross-collaboration and pushing the boundaries of what was scientifically possible.

Parallel to the Hyperloop concept, another ambitious venture emerged from Musk's desire to solve transportation challenges: The Boring Company. Musk recognized that one of the major hurdles in creating efficient transportation systems was congestion on existing road networks. He believed that by taking transportation underground, he could alleviate traffic congestion and create a more efficient way for people to travel.

The Boring Company's mission was to dig tunnels under major cities to create a network of underground transport routes. By using advanced tunneling techniques and robotics, Musk aimed to reduce the cost and time associated with tunnel construction. This innovative approach to tunneling involved the use of tunnel boring machines (TBMs) that could excavate the ground while reinforcing the tunnel walls simultaneously. The goal was to create a vast underground network that could be used not only for transportation but also for utilities and other infrastructure needs, thus maximizing the use of underground space.

Critics initially dismissed Musk's ideas as impractical and overly ambitious. They raised concerns about the safety and feasibility of the Hyperloop and questioned the viability of tunneling on such a large scale. However, as The Boring Company started to demonstrate its capabilities by successfully digging tunnels in California and Las Vegas, skepticism gradually gave way to recognition of its potential. Musk's ability to think outside the box and his relentless pursuit of innovation began to reshape the public's perception of what was possible in the realm of transportation infrastructure.

As both the Hyperloop and The Boring Company gained momentum, collaborations and partnerships with governments and private entities emerged. These collaborations aimed to further push the boundaries of technology, regulation, and cross-disciplinary research. Researchers and engineers continued to explore new materials, propulsion systems, and safety measures to make the Hyperloop a reality.

The Hyperloop's potential extends far beyond passenger transportation. It has the capacity to revolutionize the movement of goods, transforming the logistics industry on a global scale. By enabling high-speed cargo transport, the Hyperloop has the potential to streamline supply chains and significantly reduce delivery times. This innovation would have profound implications for industries such as e-commerce, manufacturing, and healthcare, where fast and efficient transportation is crucial.

The Boring Company, on the other hand, worked closely with city planners and architects to integrate their underground infrastructure with existing urban landscapes seamlessly. By creating an extensive underground network, The Boring Company sought to enable faster, quieter, and more environmentally friendly modes of transportation. This underground transportation system would have the potential to connect cities, suburbs, and even entire regions, facilitating easier access to employment, education, and recreational opportunities.

The progress made by both the Hyperloop and The Boring Company is not without its challenges. Developing novel transportation infrastructure requires overcoming technological, regulatory, and economic barriers. However, the unwavering dedication and persistence of Musk, his team, and the broader research community have pushed these ambitious projects closer to becoming reality.

As governments and policymakers recognize the potential of the Hyperloop and underground transportation, they have started actively exploring the necessary legislative frameworks and regulations. This initiative aims to ensure the safe implementation of these transformative technologies while fostering innovation and competition.

The successful realization of the Hyperloop and The Boring Company's vision would bring transformative change to the way we travel and perceive transportation infrastructure. It would not only enhance connectivity between cities but also redefine urban planning, optimize resource utilization, and reduce carbon emissions. The potential impact extends beyond transportation itself, influencing various sectors of the economy and improving the quality of life for millions of people worldwide.

Elon's audacious ideas have sparked a new era of innovation in the transportation industry. The Hyperloop and The Boring Company revolutionize the concepts of speed, efficiency, and sustainability. As these ventures evolve, they stand as testaments to Musk's unwavering belief in the power of technology to reshape our world and shape the future of transportation. This chapter captures merely a glimpse of the vast possibilities that lie ahead in the exciting realms of the Hyperloop and underground transportation infrastructure.

Chapter Nine

Neuralink and The Quest for Artificial Intelligence

D eep in cutting-edge technology and scientific innovation lies Neuralink, a project that holds the key to unlocking the mysteries of the human brain. Spearheaded by Elon Musk, Neuralink aims to create a seamless union between humans and artificial intelligence through the development of a brain-machine interface.

The quest for artificial intelligence has been a long-standing fascination for Musk. He believes that harnessing the potential of AI can elevate humanity and mitigate the risks that may arise from its exponential growth. With Neuralink, Musk envisions a future where humans can merge their cognitive abilities with AI systems, achieving unparalleled levels of cognition, creativity, and problem-solving.

Neuralink relies on a revolutionary technology known as high-bandwidth brain-machine interface (BMI). The core of this technology lies in the ultra-high-density electrode arrays that Neuralink has developed. These tiny, flexible threads, thinner than a human hair, are implanted into the brain to establish communication and interaction with neural networks at an unprecedented level of precision.

The potential applications of Neuralink are vast and varied. In the field of medicine, revolutionary breakthroughs are at the forefront. By interfacing directly with the brain, Neuralink could potentially revolutionize the treatment of neurological disorders. Patients with conditions like Alzheimer's or Parkinson's could regain lost functions, improve memory, and enhance motor control. Similarly, individuals with spinal cord injuries may find hope in the restoration of mobility through the integration of Neuralink technology.

Beyond medical applications, Neuralink has the power to transform our everyday lives. The high-bandwidth BMI technology could enable seamless interaction between humans and external devices, eliminating the need for physical interfaces. Communication through thought alone may soon become a reality, revolutionizing the way we connect with each other and the world around us.

Imagine a world where you can effortlessly control your environment with your mind. Dim your lights, adjust the temperature, or even navigate complex virtual reality environments with a mere thought. With Neuralink, this future may not be too far away. The potential for human-machine symbiosis is immense, extending far beyond the realm of medical benefits.

Expanding further into the potential of Neuralink, imagine the possibilities for education and learning. With direct access to vast knowledge databases and AI algorithms, individuals could acquire information and process complex data at unimaginable speeds. Students could learn subjects with unparalleled efficiency, accelerating the advancement of human knowledge and understanding.

However, Neuralink is not merely limited to augmenting existing human abilities. Musk envisions a future where humans can tap into the vast intelligence and computational power of AI systems, expanding the boundaries of human thought. Through Neuralink, individuals could access information, process complex data, and solve problems at unimaginable speeds, all with the power of thought.

Amidst the immense potential of Neuralink, ethical considerations loom large. Privacy, security, and the possibility of unintended consequences demand careful attention. Musk recognizes these concerns and emphasizes a safe and responsible approach towards the development of Neuralink technology. He advocates for regulatory frameworks and collaborative efforts to ensure that the benefits of Neuralink are shared by all while mitigating potential risks.

As Neuralink continues to push the boundaries of what is possible, the world eagerly awaits the realization of this transformative technology. Elon Musk, a visionary leader in the field, drives Neuralink's mission forward, guided by the belief that the merging of human minds with machines is not only possible but crucial for the advancement of humanity. The quest for artificial intelligence takes another momentous stride forward with Neuralink at its helm, illuminating a future where humans and AI coexist harmoniously, unlocking the full potential of our minds. This fusion of human and machine intelligence holds the promise of conquering new frontiers, driving forward scientific discoveries, and shaping a future where humanity thrives alongside advanced artificial intelligence.

Chapter Ten

A Journey to Mars: SpaceX's Ambitious Plan for Colonization

One of Elon's most daring and ambitious projects is the colonization of Mars through SpaceX. Musk's fascination with Mars began at a young age, fueled by his love for science fiction and the potential for exploration beyond Earth's boundaries. As he gained success in his various ventures, from PayPal to Tesla, his dream of making humanity a multiplanetary species became more tangible.

Musk firmly believes that Earth may not be able to sustain humanity forever, and he envisions Mars as a potential backup planet, ensuring the survival of our species even in the face of catastrophic events. To achieve this, SpaceX has set its sights on developing the necessary technologies and infrastructure to transport humans to Mars and establish sustainable colonies.

The chapter starts by exploring SpaceX's initial steps towards achieving this monumental goal. We delve into the development of the Falcon rockets, which became instrumental in making space travel more affordable and accessible. Musk's relentless pursuit of reusable rocket technology and his unwavering belief in its potential to drastically reduce the cost of space travel are highlighted. This breakthrough not only disrupted the traditional space industry but also paved the way for more ambitious projects like Mars colonization.

Next, we delve into the monumental undertaking of building the Interplanetary Transport System (ITS), later renamed Starship, the colossal spacecraft designed to transport humans and cargo to Mars. Its revolutionary design, coupled with the use of methane as a propellant, has the potential to significantly reduce costs and make long-duration interplanetary journeys a reality. Musk's vision for Starship goes beyond Mars colonization; he aims to use it for various missions, including satellite deployment, lunar missions, and even trips to other destinations within our solar system.

However, no endeavor of this magnitude is without its challenges and skeptics. The chapter also explores the major obstacles faced by SpaceX's Mars colonization plans. Critics argue that the technology required for Mars colonization is yet to be fully developed, and that the risks involved are immense. Questions arise about the long-term sustainability of colonies on Mars and the potential health risks posed to humans in the harsh Martian environment. Musk's bold timeline for launching crewed missions to Mars has drawn skepticism from some quarters, who argue that such a feat may take decades, if not longer, to achieve.

Despite these challenges, Musk remains undeterred. His drive to push the boundaries of what is possible and his commitment to advancing humanity's understanding of the cosmos fuels his determination to make Mars colonization a reality. The chapter delves into the ongoing research and development efforts conducted by SpaceX to address these challenges and mitigate risks.

SpaceX and Musk understand that radiation poses significant health risks to astronauts on the journey to and the surface of Mars. Therefore, to ensure the survival of future Martian colonists, the company is actively developing advanced radiation shielding technologies. These innovations aim to protect astronauts from harmful space radiation, which is of greater concern beyond Earth's protective atmosphere and magnetosphere.

Furthermore, sustainable living arrangements and advanced life support systems are being designed to tackle another pressing challenge of Mars colonization. SpaceX is exploring ways to develop closed-loop systems that minimize resource consumption and waste generation, ensuring the long-term sustainability of Martian colonies. Efforts are underway to harness the region's abundant carbon dioxide, which constitutes the majority of Mars' atmosphere, to generate essential resources like fuel, water, and oxygen through processes such as Sabatier reaction and electrolysis.

Moreover, the successful colonization of Mars holds immense societal and scientific potential. The chapter explores the potential benefits that could arise from a thriving Martian colony, including the establishment of a new frontier for human civilization, the advancement of scientific knowledge through Martian research, and the potential to inspire new technologies and industries.

The Martian environment, with its unique geological features and history, offers scientists an unprecedented opportunity to unlock the mysteries of our solar system's formation and evolution. Mars' intriguing geological formations, evidence of ancient water, and the potential for past or even present life make it a veritable treasure trove of discoveries waiting to be made. Understanding the planet's history could shed light on Earth's past, its own potential for life, and our place in the universe.

Additionally, the successful establishment of sustainable habitats on Mars can lead to breakthroughs in sustainable resource management, renewable energy, and interplanetary travel. Technologies developed for Martian colonization, such as advanced life support systems, closed-loop recycling, and efficient resource utilization, can be adapted and applied on Earth to address our own environmental challenges. The innovations spurred by Mars colonization could have far-reaching implications for sustainable living on our home planet.

As the chapter concludes, readers gain a deeper understanding of Elon Musk's audacious plan to colonize Mars and the role that SpaceX plays in achieving this monumental feat. The Journey to Mars represents a testament to Musk's determination and relentless pursuit of pushing boundaries, making it one of the most exciting and dynamic projects in the history of space exploration. Through perseverance, innovation, and a steadfast belief in the potential of humanity, Elon Musk and

SpaceX stand at the forefront of paving the way towards a multiplanetary future.

Chapter Eleven

Turbulence and Triumph: Navigating Challenges and Controversies

Throughout his career, Elon has encountered numerous challenges and controversies that have tested his resilience, ingenuity, and determination. This chapter delves even deeper into some of the most notable instances where Musk had to navigate turbulent waters in order to achieve his audacious ambitions and leave an indelible mark on the world.

The early days of SpaceX were rife with setbacks and failures that threatened to derail Musk's ambitious vision of affordable space travel. Rockets exploded during test flights, funding became scarce, and the odds seemed stacked against the young aerospace company. But Musk's unyielding determination and refusal to accept defeat propelled SpaceX forward. Through relentless problem-solving, meticulous engineering, and unwavering faith in the ingenuity of his team, Musk guided SpaceX toward its first successful launch. This groundbreaking achievement not only demonstrated the viability of privately-funded space exploration but also established Musk as a force to be reckoned with in the aerospace industry.

However, as SpaceX moved towards more ambitious goals, the challenges grew in scale and complexity. Musk's audacious plan to develop reusable rockets and drastically reduce the cost of space travel was met with skepticism and doubt. Many deemed it an impossible feat. But Musk's unwavering belief in the power of innovation and a relentless pursuit of perfection brought him closer to his goal. SpaceX endured multiple failed attempts at landing rockets, but each failure was seen as an opportunity to learn, iterate, and improve. Finally, in December 2015, the Falcon 9 rocket made a historic vertical landing, revolutionizing the space industry and demonstrating the potential for significant cost savings in future space missions.

Similarly, Tesla Motors faced its own share of controversies as it sought to revolutionize the automotive industry with sustainable electric vehicles. Critics often scoffed at the idea of mass-market electric cars, questioning their practicality, affordability, and range limitations. Traditional automotive dealerships and entrenched interests posed legal challenges to Tesla's direct sales model, attempting to stifle its growth. Musk faced these obstacles head-on, relentlessly advocating for electric vehicles and battling against restrictive dealership laws. At one point, the company teetered on the brink of bankruptcy, despite the critical acclaim received by its flagship Model S sedan. But Musk's tenacity and relentless pursuit of funding saved Tesla from imminent collapse. By securing critical investments from venture capitalists and leveraging his personal wealth, he not only kept the company afloat but also pushed forward the development of the more affordable Model 3, poised to penetrate the mass market.

But the challenges faced by Musk have not been confined to the realms of business and technology alone. His unfiltered and unapologetic nature on social media platforms, particularly Twitter, has stirred both admiration and controversy. Musk's provocative behavior and off-the-cuff remarks often ignite debates, with supporters applauding his honesty and transparent communication, while detractors accuse him of being impulsive and reckless. Yet, it is through this unfiltered nature that Musk has consistently connected with a wide audience, demonstrating his authenticity and fueling a passionate community of fans who resonate with his daring vision of the future.

Beyond the professional sphere, Musk's personal life has been marred by turmoil and public scrutiny. High-profile divorces and custody battles have thrust his private affairs into the media spotlight, adding another layer of complexity to his already hectic lifestyle. Balancing the demands of an ambitious career with personal relationships and family obligations is an ongoing challenge that Musk tackles with immense introspection and perseverance. By continuously reevaluating and refining his priorities, he strives to strike a delicate equilibrium that enables him to drive his ventures forward while nurturing meaningful connections with loved ones.

The ability to navigate challenges and controversies with resilience and adaptability has proven to be a defining characteristic of Elon Musk's trajectory. By embracing failures as valuable learning experiences rather than insurmountable obstacles, Musk has continually pushed the boundaries of what is possible in space exploration, sustainable energy, and transportation. He has shown time and again that setbacks are not synonyms for defeat but rather steppingstones to future triumphs.

Chapter Twelve

Musk: The Man Behind the Myth

Behind every successful individual lies a story of struggle, determination, and unwavering ambition. Elon Musk, a name that resonates with innovation and disruption, is no exception. In this chapter, we delve into the life and persona of the man behind the myth.

Born on June 28, 1971, in Pretoria, South Africa, Musk displayed early signs of his exceptional intellect and futuristic thinking. As a child, he was known for his insatiable curiosity and desire to understand the world around him. Musk's parents recognized his brilliance and supported his early interests, fostering an environment of intellectual stimulation and continuous learning. His father, Errol Musk, an engineer, played a vital role in nurturing Elon's innate talent and encouraging his voracious appetite for knowledge.

Musk's journey to becoming the influential entrepreneur we know today was not without its challenges. Growing up in South Africa during apartheid, he experienced both the privilege of his upper-middle-class background and the social divides that plagued his country. These early experiences fostered a strong sense of empathy and a deep desire for societal change within Musk. Additionally, Musk's early interest in computers and technology provided a means of escape and a pathway to a future he could strive for.

After completing his studies in South Africa, Musk made a bold decision to pursue his dreams in the United States. Arriving in California, the heart of innovation, Musk sought to make his mark on the world. His first venture, Zip2, revolutionized the online business directory industry, laying the foundation for his future endeavors. Zip2's success not only showcased Musk's entrepreneurial acumen but also his ability to identify gaps in the market and develop innovative solutions.

Although Zip2 achieved considerable success, it was Musk's involvement with X.com, which later became known as PayPal, that propelled him into the realm of global recognition. PayPal's vision of creating a secure and accessible online payment system aligned with Musk's own mission to revolutionize industries and change lives. Musk's role in PayPal's success provided him with the financial resources and credibility to pursue his wildest ambitions.

However, it was the founding of SpaceX in 2002 that truly solidified Musk's status as a visionary. Breaking into the heavily regulated and risk-averse aerospace industry was no small feat, but Musk's unwavering belief in the potential of space exploration drove him to push boundaries and challenge conventional wisdom. With SpaceX, Musk aimed not only to revolutionize space travel but also to make it more accessible and affordable for future generations.

Tesla Motors, another groundbreaking venture by Musk, aimed to change the perception of electric vehicles and redefine the future of transportation. Combining innovation, sustainability, and luxury, Tesla quickly became synonymous with cutting-edge technology and advanced engineering, capturing the imagination of consumers worldwide. Musk's dedication to sustainability extended beyond electric vehicles, as he also championed the creation of the Gigafactory, a facility focused on producing sustainable energy solutions at scale.

Beyond his entrepreneurial pursuits, Musk has also made headlines for his audacious ambitions, such as the Hyperloop transportation concept and Neuralink's quest for merging human brains with artificial intelligence. These ventures reflect Musk's unrelenting commitment to pushing the boundaries of what is possible and his relentless pursuit of a brighter, more innovative future.

However, behind the scenes, Musk's personal life has faced its own challenges. Known for his intense work ethic and demanding leadership style, Musk has often been criticized for his management practices and occasional public controversies. Yet, amidst the public scrutiny, Musk continues to push forward, unyielding in his pursuit of his goals.

As we peel back the layers, we discover a man whose relentless drive and ambition are tempered by vulnerability and humanity. Musk's personal life has seen its share of triumphs and setbacks, love, and heartbreak. His first marriage to Justine Wilson lasted for eight years, during which they had six children, but they eventually divorced. Musk's second marriage to British actress Talulah Riley ended in divorce as well, although they remarried and subsequently divorced again.

Musk's relationship with his five sons has been an important aspect of his life. He has openly discussed the challenges of balancing his demanding work schedule with being a present father, but he remains committed to nurturing their growth and instilling in them a similar sense of curiosity and ambition. Musk's commitment to his children has been reflected in initiatives such as Ad Astra, a school he founded for his children and other select students, aimed at providing a unique educational experience focused on critical thinking and problem-solving.

Chapter Thirteen

The Work-Life Balancing Act: Elon Musk's Personal Life

While Musk's dedication to his work is undeniable, he also recognizes the importance of nurturing his personal life. He understands that achieving a harmonious balance requires intentional efforts and a mindful approach. Even though he has often been described as a workaholic, he continually strives to find equilibrium and prioritize his relationships and well-being.

As a devoted father, Musk cherishes the time he spends with his six children, valuing the deep bond he shares with each one of them. Despite his demanding schedule, he makes it a point to be actively present in their lives. Musk acknowledges that children grow up quickly and realizes that the time he spends with them is precious. From taking them to school and assisting with homework to engaging in meaningful conversations, he fosters an open and supportive environment that allows them to thrive.

To ensure he is available for his children's important moments, Musk has established strict boundaries when it comes to work. He dedicates specific days and times solely for family activities and ensures that work-related distractions do not encroach upon these sacred hours. Musk believes that nurturing healthy family relationships is critical for his personal well-being as well as for the growth and happiness of his children.

In addition to his commitment to his children, Musk understands the significance of maintaining a healthy lifestyle. He acknowledges that physical and mental wellness is essential to sustain his demanding pace and undertake the colossal challenges he and his companies face. Musk engages in regular exercise, adhering to a strict fitness regimen that includes daily workouts, hikes in the scenic outdoors, and participation in extreme sports like skydiving and scuba diving. These adrenaline-pumping activities not only provide him with the necessary physical exertion but also serve as a source of mental clarity, enabling him to tackle complex problems with a fresh perspective.

To effectively manage his vast array of responsibilities, Musk understands the importance of delegation and building a supportive team. While he possesses an exceptional ability to tackle a broad range of tasks, he acknowledges that he cannot shoulder the entire workload on his own. By surrounding himself with talented individuals who share his vision and ambition, Musk is able to delegate tasks, entrusting his team to handle various aspects of his organizations. This strategic approach not only relieves some of the burden from him but also allows him to dedicate time for personal endeavors and nurturing his relationships.

Musk also practices mindfulness and introspection to maintain a healthy work-life balance. He takes time for activities such as meditation and journaling, which serve as outlets for self-reflection and relaxation. This introspective practice allows him to remain grounded in the present moment, enabling him to prioritize his personal life even in the midst of demanding work commitments.

Despite Musk's unwavering commitment to finding a work-life balance, he openly acknowledges that it can be an ongoing challenge. When confronted with critical moments or significant obstacles, he may find himself pulled more towards work and facing difficulty in maintaining equilibrium. However, he is committed to constantly reassessing his priorities and making necessary adjustments to ensure that his personal life remains a fundamental pillar in his journey.

Chapter Fourteen

Leadership Lessons: Insights from Musk's Innovative Style

One of the most striking aspects of Musk's leadership style is his unwavering belief in his vision and his ability to effectively communicate it to his team. Musk possesses a rare combination of confidence and charisma that enables him to rally his employees behind his ambitious goals. He not only shares his vision with passion but also ensures that it is understood on a fundamental level by his team members. Musk's communication style is characterized by clarity and transparency, as he establishes an open dialogue where ideas and feedback are welcomed. By fostering a culture of open communication, Musk ensures that his employees feel empowered to contribute their insights and perspectives, further enriching the collaborative environment.

Furthermore, Musk's leadership is rooted in a strong sense of purpose. He believes in using innovation and technology to tackle some of the world's most pressing challenges. Whether it is the pursuit of sustainable energy through electric vehicles and renewable energy sources or the exploration of space to ensure the survival of humanity, each of Musk's ventures is driven by a greater purpose. This purpose-driven approach to leadership instills a sense of meaning and fulfillment within the workforce, enabling them to feel aligned with something larger than themselves. By clarifying the purpose behind their work, Musk taps into the intrinsic motivations of his employees, fueling their passion and dedication.

A key leadership lesson we can learn from Musk is his insistence on hiring the best talent and creating a high-performance culture. He understands that his companies can only thrive if they have the right people in place, and he leaves no stone unturned in his quest for top talent. Musk's recruitment process is rigorous, as he seeks individuals who not only possess exceptional skill sets but also demonstrate a hunger for knowledge and a deep curiosity about the world. He values diversity and actively seeks out different perspectives and backgrounds to foster innovation and creativity within his teams. Moreover, Musk places a strong emphasis on cultivating a culture of excellence by setting high standards and encouraging continuous learning and improvement. This high-performance culture drives his employees to push boundaries, challenge assumptions, and consistently deliver exceptional results.

Musk also demonstrates a willingness to take calculated risks and embrace failure as a part of the learning process. He understands that innovation requires experimentation and that setbacks are inevitable. Rather than being discouraged by failure, Musk uses it as an opportunity to iterate and improve. His resilience and ability to bounce back from adversity serve as a powerful example for his employees. This approach to failure not only fosters a culture of continuous learning and adaptation but also encourages his team to think creatively and take calculated risks themselves. By creating an environment where failure is not stigmatized but seen as a necessary step on the path to success, Musk empowers his employees to push boundaries and pursue ambitious goals.

In addition to his visionary leadership and risk-taking, Musk also possesses a relentless work ethic and attention to detail. He leads by example, working long hours and setting high standards for himself and his team. Musk's dedication to his craft and pursuit of excellence are contagious, inspiring those around him to give their best effort. This level of commitment not only drives his team to go above and beyond but also ensures that he remains intimately involved in the day-to-day operations of his companies. Musk's operational involvement allows him to make informed decisions, troubleshoot challenges, and provide guidance to his teams based on a deep understanding of the technical aspects of each business.

Furthermore, Musk's leadership style is characterized by a long-term, big-picture mindset. He is not afraid to challenge conventional wisdom and disrupt established industries. Musk's ability to think in terms of decades rather than short-term gains has allowed him to take bold risks and drive innovation. Rather than being solely focused on quarterly earnings or immediate market trends, Musk embraces a long-term perspective. He anticipates future needs and endeavors to create innovative solutions that will have enduring impact. This forward-thinking perspective inspires his employees to think expansively, consider alternative approaches, and strive for long-term sustainable success.

Musk's leadership style is also marked by a continuous pursuit of knowledge and personal growth. He is known for voraciously consuming books across various disciplines to expand his understanding of the world. This thirst for knowledge allows him to connect seemingly unrelated concepts and apply them to his businesses. Musk encourages his employees to adopt a similar mindset by providing opportunities for learning and development. Whether through workshops, conferences, or internal knowledge-sharing sessions, Musk ensures that his workforce has access to resources and experiences that allow them to grow both personally and professionally. This commitment to ongoing learning not only boosts the individual capabilities of his team members but also enhances the overall intellectual capacity of his organizations.

Chapter Fifteen

Reflection and Future Outlook: Elon Musk's Impact and Continued Vision

As the book nears its conclusion, it is essential to reflect on Elon's remarkable impact and contemplate the future of his endeavors. Musk's influence reaches far beyond the realms of business and technology, inspiring a generation of visionaries to dream bigger and reach for the stars.

Elon Musk's accomplishments have revolutionized several industries, including transportation, energy, space travel, and beyond. His relentless pursuit of sustainable and innovative solutions has propelled him to the forefront of technological innovation, earning him a place among the most influential figures of our time and a reputation as a modern-day Renaissance man.

Perhaps one of Musk's most significant accomplishments is his role in transforming the electric vehicle industry. With Tesla Motors, he reimagined the concept of electric cars, shaping them into sleek, high-performance vehicles that have captivated consumers worldwide. Musk saw the potential of electric vehicles to combat climate change and reduce dependence on fossil fuels, and he turned that vision into a reality. Tesla's commitment to sustainability extends beyond just the vehicles themselves, with the construction of an extensive network of supercharger stations for convenient and efficient long-distance travel. Alongside this goal, Tesla's innovative battery technology has also gained attention, not only powering electric vehicles but also revolutionizing energy storage systems for homes and businesses. This progress has led to significant advancements in grid-level energy storage, facilitating the integration of renewable energy sources and helping to create a more resilient and sustainable power grid.

Furthermore, Musk's foray into space exploration with SpaceX has revitalized global interest in interplanetary travel. Musk's overarching vision is to make humanity a multi-planetary species, and SpaceX's achievements are crucial milestones in realizing this future. The successful launch and landing of reusable rockets have proven that space travel can be economically viable and sustainable. Musk's bold vision for a multi-planetary society has captured the world's imagination, with plans to establish a self-sustaining colony on Mars within our lifetime. This ambitious endeavor has sparked renewed interest and collaboration in the space industry, reigniting humanity's dream of exploring the cosmos. SpaceX's ongoing partnership with NASA to transport astronauts to the International Space Station and the development of the Starship, a fully reusable spacecraft, further exemplify Musk's commitment to advancing space exploration. The potential for interplanetary travel and colonization has the potential to not only ensure the survival of humanity but also to unlock vast new opportunities for scientific discovery and expansion of our civilization.

In addition to his endeavors in transportation and space, Musk's ventures in renewable energy, such as SolarCity, have further solidified his commitment to a sustainable future. By harnessing the power of the sun and developing efficient battery storage, Musk aims to reshape the energy landscape and accelerate the transition to clean energy sources. SolarCity's innovative solar panel technologies, combined with Tesla's energy storage solutions, provide a comprehensive approach to sustainable power generation and utilization. Beyond residential and commercial applications, Tesla's focus on utility-scale energy storage installations has the potential to revolutionize the way we capture and store renewable energy on a large scale. These advancements not only contribute to reducing carbon emissions and combatting climate change but also hold the promise of energy independence and stability for communities around the world.

Looking to the future, Elon Musk's impact is set to expand further. His involvement with Neuralink exemplifies his relentless pursuit of innovation in the field of brain-machine interfaces. Musk envisions a future where humans can augment their cognitive abilities and potentially overcome neurological disorders through direct interfaces with computers. Neuralink's development of high-bandwidth brain-machine interfaces has the potential to revolutionize healthcare, communication, and human capabilities as we know them. By enabling a direct connection between the human brain and external devices, Musk's vision of a symbiotic relationship between humans and artificial intelligence could unleash untapped potential and shape the next phase of human evolution.

Furthermore, Musk's visionary approach is not limited to his own ventures. He actively encourages collaboration and open-source initiatives in technology and scientific research. Through initiatives such as the Tesla patents being made open-source, Musk demonstrates his belief in the power of collective intelligence and collaboration. He understands that progress is accelerated when individuals and organizations work together for a common goal. This collaborative spirit has already fostered innovations and breakthroughs in various fields, and it is poised to continue driving societal advancements well into the future.

His continued vision and impact extend far beyond the scope of any one individual or company. His relentless pursuit of innovation, coupled with his dream of creating a sustainable and multi-planetary future, will undoubtedly shape the course of human history. As we reflect on his accomplishments and contemplate the future, it becomes clear that Musk's legacy will continue to shape the world for generations to come, leaving an indelible mark on humanity's quest for progress, discovery, and the realization of our greatest aspirations. With every groundbreaking achievement and audacious goal, Elon Musk inspires us to push boundaries and strive for a future where our collective potential knows no bounds.